Pilgrims Plantation

Pilgrims Plantation

By June Behrens and Pauline Brower

Photographs compiled by Pauline Brower

A Golden Gate Junior Book   Childrens Press • Chicago

ACKNOWLEDGEMENT

The authors wish to acknowledge with thanks the assistance of the Plimoth Plantation staff and the following individuals for their contribution to the preparation of the manuscript: Ted Avery and Tom Young, *Audio-Visual Staff;* Muriel Stefani, *Public Relations;* Bob Marten, *Research Staff;* and Kelley Brower.

Plimoth Plantation is an interpretive site located three miles south of Plymouth, Massachusetts. It is a living folk museum of seventeenth-century Plymouth.

Library of Congress Cataloging in Publication Data

Behrens, June.
  Pilgrims plantation.

  "A Golden Gate junior book."
  SUMMARY: Follows two children of the Plimoth Plantation through the first seven years of settlement.
    1. Plymouth, Mass.—Social life and customs— Juvenile literature. 2. Pilgrims (New Plymouth Colony) —Juvenile literature. [1. Plymouth, Mass.—History. 2. Pilgrims (New Plymouth Colony) 3. Massachusetts— History—New Plymouth, 1620-1691] I. Brower, Pauline, joint author. II. Title.
  F74.P8B44   1977   974.4'82   77-2852
  ISBN 0-516-08736-3

LAND! IT WAS THEIR first sight of land since they had left England, over two months ago. The *Mayflower* had brought them across a stormy ocean to this new world. Elizabeth reminded Daniel that it was almost Christmas. They would start the new year of 1621 in a land called America.

Elizabeth and Daniel were anxious to touch land again. But they could not leave the crowded ship, at anchor in Plimoth Harbor, until Father and the other men found the right location for their settlement.

Many times Father left the *Mayflower* with the others to board a little shallop boat. In it the men explored land along the shore, looking for a clearing on high ground near good water. Finally they agreed on just the right place to build their homes. They would call their new settlement *Plimoth Plantation*.

It was spring before Elizabeth and Daniel left the

Mayflower to live on land again. It had been a bitter winter. Many of their friends had died.

That first spring Elizabeth and Daniel worked together with all the *Mayflower* families to build their new homes. They used logs from the forest and sticks woven together, called wattle, to make the walls. They used sand, clay, water and straw mixed

together to make a daub plaster to cover the walls.

Daniel watched as the carpenter smoothed rough lumber into clapboards with a draw knife. The Pilgrims had brought the draw knife with them from England.

All the supplies and tools brought on the *Mayflower* belonged to a company the Pilgrims and a group of English merchants had formed. Everyone owned shares in everything. The merchants in England owned most of the shares. The Pilgrim families had agreed to pay the merchants for the voyage and supplies. They would send lumber, furs and other goods back to England as payment.

Daniel and Elizabeth helped to find reeds and wild grass for the roof thatcher. He put on thick thatches of grass as a roof cover to keep out snow and rain.

The chimney was made of daub and wattle. Father and Daniel replaced the daub when it fell off so that sparks would not catch the roof on fire.

That first year several families lived together until a cottage could be built for each family. Elizabeth

was used to a small space with little furniture, after staying the winter on the *Mayflower*. She and the others slept on pallets on the earthen floor. They wore their clothes to bed to keep warm.

The Pilgrim families built a high palisade fence of tall stakes around their cottages for protection. Even though friendly Indians were nearby, there was always danger from unfriendly tribes.

Friendly Indians visited the Pilgrims that first

spring. One Indian, named Squanto, spoke English. Squanto lived with the Pilgrims and helped them to plant crops and catch fish.

Squanto arranged peace talks between the Pilgrims and his chief, Massasoit. Massasoit agreed to protect them from unfriendly Indian tribes. He wanted to trade with the Pilgrims and to be their friend.

The plantation cooper was an important village

craftsman. He made hogshead barrels in which to store the trade goods to be sent back to England.

Daniel sometimes helped the cooper find the wood to make containers of different sizes. Wooden barrels and buckets were used to hold and store food. Mother carried water from the spring in buckets made by the cooper.

During those first few years, Elizabeth, Daniel and their neighbors worked together as one big family. Each person did the job he was able to do. A few women washed clothes for everyone at the plantation. Others took care of the animals. The stronger people did the heavy field work.

Fields outside the palisade fence were raked and cleared. Seeds were planted. The crop was more important than money. The families could eat the corn and use it for trading. Wheat, barley and other grains were called corn by the Pilgrims.

The Pilgrims traded their corn to the Indians for furs. The furs were valuable in England. They helped to pay the debts owed to the English merchants.

In the agreement with the English merchants, the Pilgrims and merchants owned the plantation together. Many Pilgrims did not like this agreement. They wanted to work for their own families on their own land.

As time passed, more settlers came to Plimoth Plantation. Finally the Pilgrims, with Governor

William Bradford, their elected leader, changed the rules of the agreement with the merchants in England. Each family was now given a small plot of ground for planting. But people continued to work as a group as well as in their own garden plots.

The crop production improved after each family was given its own plot of land. The families took more pride in working their own ground.

Elizabeth, Daniel and their parents, as well as all the other families, worked hard in the fields. After the ground had been raked and cleared, animal fertilizer was spread to help the seeds grow. In earlier years, before there were many animals, Squanto had taught the Pilgrims to use fish to fertilize the soil.

Governor Bradford rationed food those first years on Plimoth Plantation. He made sure that everyone had enough to eat. At first, after the long sea voyage, many people were not well enough to work. But everyone lived as a big family, sharing and helping each other.

Mother and Daniel went to the corn field in summer to pull weeds and to see how their corn was growing. When the crop was good, they knew there would be enough food for the winter months. Extra corn could be traded to the Indians for furs. After furs were sent to the merchants in England, the ship returned with more supplies for the Pilgrim families.

Mother planted a small herb garden near the cottage. Several kinds of vegetables and herbs grew in her garden. She called the vegetables herbs too.

Daniel helped to build a fence around the herb garden to keep out the animals. Each year trade ships brought more animals to the plantation.

Every fall Daniel helped store the hay crop to keep it dry for the animals to eat during the winter. The first animals shipped to the plantation were the property of the company. Later, each family owned animals.

It was a big event when a new animal was born. This was because there had been so few animals during those first years of settlement. Mother took care of the goats. The plantation cattle supplied the Pilgrims with meat, milk, butter and cheese.

Elizabeth had the special job of dividing the milk for all the families. She and Daniel started doing the work of grownups when they were six years old. All Pilgrim children worked as soon as they were old enough to learn a task from their mothers and fathers. Always the chores were many on the plantation.

In winter, before the heavy snowfalls, grandfather helped to herd the sheep to grazing land. The sheep and cattle ate the wild grasses growing around the

cottages and outside the palisade. Wool from the sheep was used to stuff the pillows and pallets Elizabeth and Daniel slept on.

Father and his neighbors made their own nets in which to catch fish. Making nets was a good wintertime activity. Father had extra time when there were no crops to tend.

Before the families sailed to America, the English merchants and Pilgrims had thought fish would be a good trade item. But the Pilgrims learned that growing corn to trade with the Indians for furs was more profitable.

In spring, Father and Daniel fished in a stream near the plantation. Squanto had shown them a good place to catch fish.

During the first years, when the crops were poor, fish was almost all people had to eat.

When the families had a good day of fishing, they salted and packed their catch in hogshead barrels. Salt preserved the fish for winter food.

One of the first things the Pilgrims brought ashore from the *Mayflower* was a cannon. The men knew it was a necessary weapon to defend themselves and to look strong.

When they first arrived, Father helped mount the cannon on top of a hill overlooking the plantation site. Later, when the fort meeting house was built, the cannon was moved to the top of the fort.

After several cottages had been built, the men constructed a redoubt defense post in the middle of the village. Men inside the redoubt could see up and

down the two streets of the village. The Pilgrims wanted to be prepared for attacks by unfriendly Indians or white men arriving on sailing ships from other countries.

When Daniel was old enough, he marched in drills with the men of the village. The men practiced drilling so they would be ready for an enemy attack.

Part of the drill was learning to fire muskets. All men worked together in preparation for defense of the plantation.

The cannon, muskets and drills made the Pilgrims

look strong to the unfriendly Indians. The plantation was not attacked during the first seven years.

When it was Father's turn to stand watch at the gates of the palisade, he was called a door ward. He opened the gates to the friendly Indians who came to visit and to trade furs. Squanto interpreted when the Pilgrims and Indians talked together.

Inside the fort there was a large room used as a meeting house. Mother and Father went to the

meetings to help make the laws for the village. Trials were held when someone broke a law. Governor Bradford helped judge the lawbreakers. Punishment for breaking a law might be a fine of money, time in the stocks, or both.

A lawbreaker sat outside in the stocks where others could see him taking his punishment. This was very embarrassing to the culprit. A person who sat in the stocks for hours would probably think twice about breaking the law a second time.

Mother and Father went to the meeting house to read the Bible and give thanks to God for their new home. The meeting house was sometimes used as a church. A few of the Pilgrims, called Separatists, believed that church was in the hearts of the people instead of in a building.

26

Harvest time was a special time for Elizabeth and Daniel and all the plantation families. Everyone joined in to help with harvesting the ripe barley and corn for winter food and trade.

When the corn was harvested, it was shucked and dried. The dried corn could be ground into meal for bread and other foods.

After harvest, Elizabeth and Daniel helped to get ready for winter. Wood was the only fuel the Pilgrims had to heat their cottages. They used wood the year around to cook their food.

Food was usually cooked in the cottage fireplace. But on a feast day Elizabeth helped with cooking outside. The Pilgrims celebrated with a feast after each harvest.

Elizabeth and Daniel would never forget the first feast they celebrated after landing in America. Because Squanto and other Indians had helped the Pilgrims grow their first crop, Massasoit, Squanto

and many of their tribe were invited to join them in celebrating this time of thanksgiving.

Massasoit brought venison and wild turkey to the first feast. Pilgrims and Indians celebrated for three days with feasting and games. There was food aplenty this time.

Mother, Father, Elizabeth and Daniel left their chores to join the other families at feasting time. The

Pilgrims gave thanks to God for the food they had grown and for their homes in the New World.

Everyone played games during the harvest celebration. The games lasted for hours. It was a joyous way to end a summer of hard work on Plimoth Plantation.

After seven years, the plantation village had grown to number thirty cottages. The people had outgrown their plantation.

It was time for a new agreement. Each person was given twenty acres of land to farm. Everything the company owned was divided among the people.

Cottages were built away from the plantation village. People wanted to live on the land they owned. New villages sprang up as more settlers came.

Elizabeth and Daniel and their neighbors were proud to be a part of the beginning of the Massachusetts colony in America.

Land at last! It had been more than two months since the *Mayflower* had set sail from England. Now the perilous crossing was over and the valiant little band of weary voyagers could begin their new life in a new world. This charming book tells the time-honored story of the Pilgrims' first settlement on the rock-bound shores of New England—but in a new way. Specially written for primary grade children, it is profusely illustrated with color photographs taken "on location" at Plimoth Plantation, Massachusetts, a present-day historical site maintained as a living folk museum of 17th century Plymouth. The easy-to-read text and graphic pictures re-create those momentous years in the life of the little colony—from the building of the first log cottages, the planting of crops, hunting and fishing, trade with the friendly Indians, to the feasts that celebrated each harvest-time, beginning with the famous First Thanksgiving in 1621. *Pilgrims Plantation* is the third book in the authors' *Living History* series, preceded by *Colonial Farm* and *Algonquian Indians At Summer Camp*, previously published.

JUNE BEHRENS has long had a notable dual career as an author of many books for youngest readers and as a distinguished educator. Born in Southern California, she took her undergraduate work at the University of California at Santa Barbara, then obtained a Master's degree in Administration from the University of Southern California. She also holds a Credential in Early Childhood Education. For many years a reading specialist in one of California's largest public school systems, Mrs. Behrens has a wealth of experience in dealing with the needs and preferences of today's young readers. Her knowledge is reflected in her many books, published by Childrens Press, ranging in subject matter from colonial history to the metric system. She is also the author of three plays for young children, *The Christmas Magic-Wagon, A New Flag For A New Country* and *Feast Of Thanksgiving*.

PAULINE BROWER'S abiding interest in our early American heritage quite naturally led her to an exploration of the many national historical interpretive sites which exist today in various parts of this country. Her enthusiasm for the rich resources she discovered at each site resulted in a collaboration with June Behrens to produce books for young readers which would give them a true sense of what America was like during its earliest beginnings. A native Californian, Mrs. Brower now lives in McLean, Virginia, near Turkey Run Farm, the scene of *Colonial Farm*, the authors' first book in their *Living History* series.